STEEL

QUALITY

QUESTION AND ANSWER

Preface

The aim of this book is to be a hand book for any mechanical engineer, civil engineer, or metallurgical engineer who is working in the steel industries. As it is the main issue in the mind of engineers during the application how to understand the quality of steel and weather the chosen steel fulfill the application-specific quality of steel.

On the other hand this hand book will also help the steel smelter continuous casting machine operator, steel quality inspector and steel producer to produce quality steel as per the application requirements.

About Author

Subhankar Pal is a Mechanical Engineer. He has completed B.Tech in Mechanical Engineering from WBUT, Kolkata. He is an experienced professional working in integrated steel plant as a Mechanical Engineer in Steel Making Division. He is post graduate certified in Steel Quality for secondary refining and continuous casting by IIT Madras.

Subhankar Pal

Email- subhankar2008.pal@gmail.com

QUESTIONS

- Clearly explain the concept of "application-specific quality of steel "
- Mention the major attributes of "good quality steel".
- What is meant by "clean steel "?
- Mention the common NMIs in steel.
- Explain the significance of "total oxygen "in steel.
- Differentiate between micro inclusions and macro inclusions. How they are measured?
- Explain the relative importance of type, amount and size of inclusions.
- Explain the limitation of primary steelmaking, and the necessity of "secondary refining "in controlling the undesirable impurities in liquid steel.
- Why "DE oxidation "or "killing "of liquid steel is essential?
- Quantitatively explain why "Al "is a better DE oxidant than "Si".
- Explain why "carried-over primary slag "is deleterious for secondary refining.
- Explain from desulphurization reaction why prior DE oxidation favors "S "removal.

- How gaseous elements "H "and "N "can be brought down in liquid steel? Explain why deoxidation and desulphurisation are essential for effective removal of "N "?
- Mention the standard secondary refining processes, and specifically explain which undesirable elements can be controlled in each process.
- **Explain how "Calcium injection "can modify melting point of inclusions of Al-oxide.**
- **Specify the roles of "Ca ", "S "and "Al "in enhancing cleanliness and cast ability.**
- **Mention the factors which favor inclusion floatation and absorption in slag of ladle.**
- **What are the common sources of large exogenous entrapments in steel?**
- **Specifically explain how "re-oxidation "of liquid steel can be minimized.**
- **Mention the steps necessary to maintain and enhance the cleanliness level in tundish.**
- **Explain the processing factors in CC mould which can impair steel cleanliness.**

- Explain why cleanliness level in cast slab / bloom is not uniform along its length and thickness.
- Clearly explain the effect of "curved mould "on distribution of inclusion along thickness of cast slab , and explain the distribution in case of " vertical mould " .
- Mention the different possible quality aberrations in cast steel.
- What are the major factors which influence the quality issues in cast steel?
- How thickness of solid shell increases with time or depth of solidification?
- Quantitatively explain the factors responsible for formation of pin holes in casting.
- Explain the parameters which control heat transfer during primary cooling in caster.

- **Explain how depth of oscillation mark is influenced by different casting parameters.**
- **How and why dendritic arm spacing changes from surface to interior of a casting?**

- Explain how to ensure desirable distribution of columnar and equiaxed cast grains.
- Explain the sequence of solidification for steels with 0.05, 0.20 and 0.60 % carbon.
- Identify at what stage transformation occurs in the above three steels.
- Explain why "S "or "P "segregates more during solidification than "Mn "or "Si ".
- How segregation changes the "actual solidus "of a steel, and the relative depths of "solid Shell "and "mushy zone" in the solidifying strand ?
- Mention the sources of strains on the cast strand during and after solidification.
- Explain the significance of " ZST " , " ZDT " and " LIT " of the strand during casting .
- Why knowledge of both strength and toughness of solidifying strand is important?
- Clearly specify the importance of "brittle zone near actual solidus "on crack formation during solidification.
- Mention how the two essential intrinsic solidification behaviors are related to actual casting factors.

- Explain why "P "is more deleterious for steel grades solidifying through γ than δ
- Explain for which carbon content strain associated with δ to γ transformation is a matter of Concern for crack formation during casting of carbon steel.
- How chemistry of a steel grade influences its intrinsic solidification characteristic?
- What are the factors responsible for generation of cracks on concast surface?
- Explain why some times undesirable "coarse cast grains "are formed.
- Specify the factors associated with the different temperature regions of brittleness.
- Mention the common internal cracks in continuous casting and their reasons.
- How bulging in cast slab can be controlled in mould, and during secondary cooling.

- Specify why steels solidifying "entirely through δ or γ "are prone to mould sticking.
- Specify the CC parameters necessary for good quality irrespective of steel grade.

- Which parameters are essential for the so-called peritectic grade with about 0.1% C?
- Explain why "mechanical soft reduction "is desirable to minimize central looseness.
- Why higher ratio (> 25) of Mn / S in steel is desirable for good quality?
- Why casting powder of different characteristics are used for AISI 430 and AISI 304.
- How the genesis of undesirable entrapments in steel can be specifically found out?
- Explain the features revealed by simple polishing and those by subsequent etching.

- o **1. Clearly explain the concept of "application-specific quality of steel "**

Quality of steel: It is the conformance to match physical and chemical attributes for specific application requirement of steel.

Different Attributes:

1. **Physical attributes**
   - Surface
   - Flatness
   - Dimensions, etc.
2. **Metallurgical attributes**
   - Proper chemical properties. (I.e. % of C, % of Fe, % of Al, etc.)
   - Range of residuals and trace elements. (I.e. <u>Residuals</u>- P, S, O, H, N. <u>Trace Elements</u>- Pb, As, Tn, Zn, etc.)
   - Minimum surface and internal defects. (I.e. cracks, lamination, silver, porosity, etc.)
   - Desirable micro structure and properties. (I.e. Grain structure, mechanical properties etc.)
   - Desired cleanliness of steel. (I.e. Inclusion size and number of inclusion should be within range.)

<u>**Application oriented quality of steel according to physical attribute:**</u>

If the surface finishes, flatness and the entire physical dimensions match according to required application of steel, this is a good quality of steel.

Application oriented quality of steel according to metallurgical attribute:

- **Chemical Properties:** If the chemical properties of steel match with the required chemical composition of steel, this is a good quality of steel.
- **Residuals:** Element P, S, N, H, O, are the residual in steel. All those residuals should be within a specified range according to the application. If all the residual are within the given range then this is a good quality of steel.
- **Trace Elements:** Trace element like Pb, As, Tn, Cu, Zn, etc. are inherited from scrap. All those elements should not be present in the steel. Steel containing minimum percent of all those trace elements are a good quality steel.
- **Surface & Internal defects:** Defects like cracks, lamination, silver, porosity should be minimum for a good quality of steel.
- **Micro structure and properties:** Grain structure, mechanical properties like elasticity etc. should match with the desired quality of steel. Then this is considered as a good quality of steel.
- **Cleanliness of Steel:** The size and number of inclusion (oxide, nitrides, sulphides) should be

within the specified range. Then this steel will be considered as a good quality of steel.

- ○ **Mention the major attributes of "good quality steel".**

The major attribute of steels are

1. **Physical Attribute:**Good quality steel should satisfy the entire physical attribute like flatness, surface quality, dimensions etc.
2. **Metallurgical Attributes:**
   - **Specified chemistry:** Good quality steel chemistry should match with the required application oriented steel chemistry (I.e. % of C, % of Fe, % of Al, etc.)
   - **Cleanliness of steel:** Good quality steel should be reasonably clean i.e. inclusion in steel should be within the limit.

   **Residual impurities: S, P, H, O, N
   NMIS: oxides, sulphide, nitrides
   Trace elements: As, Sn, Cu, Zn, etc.**

Amount, size, distribution of inclusions should not affect desired microstructure, properties, surface and internal quality.

Products	Max residual content		Max NMIS size	S	P
Deep Drawn sheet	Total O: 25PPM	N: 30PPM	100 micron	<0.005	<0.015

Steel will be accepted as good quality steel for deep drawn sheet if all this parameter match

- **Surface & Internal defects:** Surface and internal defects are generated due to inclusions present in the liquid steel. If liquid steel is not reasonable clean, many number of problem on surface and internal structure of steel.
- **Exogenous Entrapment:** It is very harmful in steel quality. They are in size of grater greater than 10 micron.

Source of exogenous entrapment- Slag from ladle, tundish, mould.

Reoxidation process - Refractory erosion

products (Aluminum oxide, Magnesium oxide)

Cleanliness and specified chemistry are the most important attribute in the quality of steel to care in metallurgical attribute.

- ○ **What is meant by "clean steel "?**

A steel will be called as clean steel when amount, chemistry, size, distribution of NMIS, residuals, trace element and exogenous entrapment is within limit, then this steel is called as clean steel.

- **Residual Impurities:** S, P, H, O, N
- **NMIS:** OXIDES, SULPHIDES, NITRIDES
- **Trace element:** As, Sn, Cu, Pb, Zn etc.
- **Exogenous entrapment:** SLAG, REOXIDATION PRODUCTS, MAGNESIUM OXIDE, CARBIDE, AL_2O_3

- **Residual Impurities:** all the residual impurities like S, P, H, O, N should be within the specified limit. Residual impurities can be controlled in different stages of steel making like BF, BOF/EAF, LRF, and VD. Residual impurities should be within limit for clean steel.
- **NMIS:** NMIS are the micro inclusion in steel. They have the influence on grain size. And they are of different mechanical properties. NMIS are the product of metallurgical process. The common NMIS are different complex oxides.

Size and distribution should be within limit for clean steel.

- **Trace Elements:** It is mainly the impurities or undesired element in the steel originated from the scrap used for steel making. Scrap is nursery for steelmaking but trace elements are undesired. Trace element only can be controlled by selection of proper scrap.
- **Exogenous entrapment:** Those are the most harmful impurities for the steel. Those are in size of much more greater than 10 micron. The sources of exogenous entrapments are slag from ladle, tundish, mold, refractory erosion and re- oxidation process.

For clean steel size and distribution of exogenous entrapment should be within specified limit.

Products	Max residual content		Max NMIS size	S	P
Deep Drawn sheet	Total O: 25PPM	N: 30PPM	100 micron	<0.005	<0.015

Steel will be said as clean steel for deep drawn sheet if all this parameter match.

Common type of non-metallic inclusions are: (a) Micro inclusion (b) Macro inclusion

(a) Micro inclusion: (size: 1 to 10 micron)
Size and distribution of NMIS decides the quality parameter of steel. This type of inclusion is mainly the product of metallurgical process **oxidation.** These types of inclusion have a strong influence on grain size, mechanical properties.

Example: Complex oxide, oxy-sulphide, sulphide, etc.

Sulphide :sulphur content of steel – Known from analysis.
Oxides:Oxygen content at final stage. – Normally not measured.
Total oxygen:It is the indicator or measure of oxygen in the steel – Dissolved oxygen + as oxide.
Total oxygen content after refining is normally taken as measure of oxide cleanliness.
Say, Total oxygen = 30 ppm, Dissolved oxygen = 5ppm,
          So oxide = 25ppm
(b) Exogenous entrapment: (size: >> 10 micron)

Common types of exogenous entrapment are **slag, re-oxidation products, and refractory erosion.**

Slag comes from ladle, tundish, mould.
Re-oxidation product is generated when steel is re- oxidized at the final stage even at the time of casting.
Refractory erosion products like magnesium oxide, carbide, aluminum oxide due to erosion of refractory from ladle, tundish, furnace refractory lining.

Large exogenous entrapment greater than 50 micron is very harmful for steel quality.

- o **Explain the significance of "total oxygen "in steel.**

In steel oxygen is present in from of dissolved oxygen and in the form of different complex oxides.

Total oxygen = Dissolved oxygen (low) + oxides

Total oxygen content after refining is normally taken as measure of oxide cleanliness of steel.

<u>**Content and size of macro (NMIS) inclusions:**</u>

- 1 KG of reasonably clean steel contains approx. 10^8 NMIS.
- 400 are of 80 to 130 micron in size.
- 10 are off 130 to 200 micron in size.
- 1 is of 200 to 270 micron in size.

Few large NMIS are harmful in quality point of view and detection of those few inclusion is very difficult

Therefore total oxygen content after final refining is taken as measure of macro cleanliness.

Products	Max residual content		Max NMIS size	S	P
Deep Drawn sheet	Total O: 25PPM	N: 30PPM	100 micron	<0.005	<0.015

Total oxygen for deep drawn sheet should be within 25 ppm.

- o **Differentiate between micro inclusions and macro inclusions. How they are measured?**

S. No	Parameter	Micro Inclusion	Macro Inclusion
1	Type of Inclusion	Endogenous	Exogenous
2	source of inclusion	Comes from chemical reaction during melting, solidification process	Comes from erosion of furnace walls are lined with refractory material, slag.
3	size	1 to 10 micron	Much more greater than 10 micron
4	Example	P,S,H,O,N	$AL2O3$, MGO, $SIO2$
5	Type of defects	cracks, porosity, hot shortness, embrittlement	interfacial crack, internal imperfection

How micro inclusions and macro inclusions are measured

- S & P analysis is a part of routine steel analysis.
- Total O and N are measured by using small machined sample.

- Micro inclusions are measured by using optical microscope.
- Macro inclusions are evaluated by slime extraction.

o Explain the relative importance of type, amount and size of inclusions.

Type, amount, and size of inclusion are very important parameter for steel cleanliness. All those parameter should be within desired limit for clean steel.

Oxide cleanliness is measured on the basis of TOTAL OXYGEN

Total oxygen = Dissolved oxygen + oxide

In case of normal grade steel **Total o: < 30 ppm;** if **total o > 40 ppm** then the steel is **downgraded.**

Cleanliness requirement for various steel products

For line pipe steel total o should be within 30ppm, nitrogen concentration should be within 30 ppm and max nonmetallic inclusion size should be 100 micron.

Similarly for tire cord steel total o should be within 15 ppm, nitrogen concentration should be within 40 ppm and max size of nonmetallic inclusion should be 15 micron.

Product	Max content	residual		Max NMI size
Line pipe	Total O: 30 ppm	N: 30 ppm		100 Micron
Deep drawn sheet	Total O: 25 ppm	N: 30 ppm		100 Micron
Heavy Plate	Total O: 20 ppm	N: 30 ppm		Cluster: 100 Micron single: 20 Micron
wire	Total O: 30 ppm	N: 60 ppm		20 Micron
Tire Cord	Total O: 15 ppm	N: 40 ppm		15 Micron
Ball Bearing	Total O: 10 ppm			15 Micron

For the stringent application of steel total O content should be less and size of inclusion should be less.

Restriction on S, P, H

Higher grade of line pipe

S<0.005, P< 0.010, H< 1.5 ppm

Deep drawn sheet

S< 0.005, P< 0.015

For higher grade of line pipe **sulphur** concentration should be **within 0.005** and **P** concentration should be **within 0.010** and good amount of degassing is needed, **hydrogen** should not be more than **1.5ppm.**

- **Explain the limitation of primary steelmaking, and the necessity of "secondary refining "in controlling the undesirable impurities in liquid steel.**

Limitation of primary steelmaking

Primary stages of steel making are BOF OR EAF OR INDUCTION FURNACE.

- Slag is rich in FeO (>20%), MnO, P_2O_5
- Liquid steel is rich in dissolved O (> 500 ppm)

Therefore

- Deoxidation is not effective as dissolves Al react with oxide present in slag so oxygen content in steel increase in liquid steel. So effective deoxidation is difficult to achieve.
- Desulphurization is not effective. As for effective desulphurization first effective deoxidation is necessary.
- Recovery of alloying elements is poor and erratic.

> Difficult to achieve close chemistry and cleanliness.

Necessity of "secondary refining "in controlling the undesirable impurities

- Narrow range of chemistry achievement.
- Homogeneous composition, Improved cleanliness

Refining and controlling

> Deoxidation (Al Killing)
> Carburisation or Decarburisation.
> Desulphurization or sulphur addition.
> Control of nitrogen and hydrogen.
> Modification of inclusion by injection of casi or café.
> Control of liquid steel temperature

o **Why "DE oxidation "or "killing "of liquid steel is essential?**

Proper deoxidation is necessary for several reason.
- If deoxidation is not effective, effective desulphurization is not possible.
- Recovery of alloying element is poor and erratic.
- Difficult to achieve close chemistry.
- Cleanliness is poor.
- Effective removal of N is not possible without proper deoxidation.

Deoxidation related to desulphurization and other parameter:

Desulphurization is a slag- metal reaction. Sulphur present in the metal react with basic rich slag CaO
Reaction: $(CaO) + [S] = (CaS) + [O]$

If deoxidation is not proper, during desulphurization reaction dissolved O in steel increase. So cleanliness of steel is affected.
And this dissolved oxygen again react with Al present in liquid steel

Hence, recovery of alloying element is poor.

Hence, it is difficult to achieve a close chemistry in steel.

As dissolved oxygen in steel increasing, total O in steel is increasing, so cleanliness of steel gets affected.

Deoxidation related to degassing:

Due to improper deoxidation S and O are more in the liquid steel. S and O are very surface active. During degassing for the presence of S and O proper N removal is not possible.

- Quantitatively explain why "Al "is a better deoxidant than "Si".

Deoxidation Reaction: $X[M] + Y[O] = (M_xO_y)$
M is any deoxidizer : Mn, Si, Al, Ca

M_xO_y is deoxidation product
Equilibrium constant $Km` = A_{MO}/ (h_M)^x (h_o)^Y$
$(W_M)^X (W_O)^Y = Km$, where $K = 1/ Km`$
 Km is constant for a temperature
At 1600 c temperature value of Km for Al and Si are
$3x10^{-14}$ and $2x10^{-5}$ respectively.

So, using the same amount of deoxidizer, soluble O will
be lower for Al than Si.

○ **Explain why "carried-over primary slag
"is deleterious for secondary refining.**

Slag carry over from primary stage to secondary stages
is deleterious as reoxidation and P reversal process
takes place.
Carried over primary slag is in rich FeO more than 20%
and P2O5.
When FeO reacts with Al and more amount of Al2O3 is
generated hence, inclusion increase and close
chemistry cannot be achieved.

And Al also reacts with P2O5 and P reversal takes
place.

**Reactions: (FeO) + [Al] = (Al$_2$O$_3$), (P$_2$O$_5$) + [Al] =
(Al$_2$O$_3$) + [P]**

**Decrease in dissolved aluminum will increase in
dissolved oxygen.**

Desulphurization is a slag- metal reaction. Sulphur present in the metal react with basic rich slag CaO
Reaction: (Cao) + [S] = (CaS) + [O]
Equilibrium constant k` = A_{cas} * h_o / A_{cao} *h_S
From this we can say the reaction will be faster if more amount of CaO present in the slag and low amount of O present in the liquid steel.
Hence we can say DE oxidation favors S removal.

Gaseous element H and N can be brought down in liquid steel by degassing process. H and N present in steel in the form of soluble H and N. For removing from steel first get transfer to surface of liquid steel then transform in hydrogen and nitrogen gas.

Reactions: [H] = ½ H_2 (g)
               [N] = ½ N_2 (g)

Activity coefficient: [h_H] = $K_H P_{h2}^{1/2}$ here
reaction depend on partial pressure.
               [h_N] = $K_N P_{n2}^{1/2}$ H   and   N
can be removed under vacuum.

<u>**Depending on K value**</u>
At 1600 c and normal atmospheric pressure (760 mm Hg): **[H] ~5ppm, [N] ~ 50ppm**
At 1 torr (1 mm Hg) :**[H] ~ 1ppm, [N] ~ 15ppm**
In reality theoretical and actual value of N removal differ because of slow kinetics, only 30% is achievable.

<u>**Necessity of proper deoxidation and desulphurization:**</u>

In case of N removal reaction takes place in three stapes
- Mass transfer of [N] in liquid steel
- Slow surface chemical reaction
- Mass transfer of N2 in the gas phase

If proper DE oxidation and desulphurization is not done then last stage gets affected. As O and S are more surface active those element retard N degassing.

- Mention the standard secondary refining processes, and specifically explain which undesirable elements can be controlled in each process.

<u>**- Common secondary refining processes:**</u>

1. LRF- Ladle refining furnace
2. IM- Injection metallurgy
3. VD- Vacuum degassing
4. VAD- Vacuum arc degassing

5. VOD- Vacuum oxygen decarburiser
6. RH- RuhrstahalHeraus degasser
7. IGP- Inert gas purging

<u>Secondary refining process and capabilities:</u>

Capability	VD	VAD	LF	VOD	IM	IGP
Deoxidation	Yes	Yes	Yes	Yes	Yes	Yes
Desulphurization	Yes	Yes	Yes	Yes	Yes	Minor
Decarburisation	No	No	No	Yes	No	No
Heating	No	Yes	Yes	Yes (Chemical)	No	No
Degassing	Yes	Yes	No	Yes	No	No
Inclusion Modification	No	Yes	Yes	No	Yes	Minor

- **Explain how "Calcium injection "can modify melting point of inclusions of Al-oxide.**

To modify the melting point of Al-Oxide inclusion we use Ca-Si or Ca-Fe wire. Ca-Si powder is encased in a steel tube. We fed this wire with the help of wire feeding machine.

<u>**Important parameters of wire feeding**</u>

- Speed of spindle of wire feeding machine
- Amount of wire is injected
- How deep it is reaching in liquid steel bath

<u>**Chemical reactions**</u>

$3[Ca] + (Al_2O_3) = 2[Al] + 3(CaO)$

Then CaO react with Al_2O_3 form Al_2O_3 – CaO compound.

From **Al_2O_3 – CaO** phase diagram we found if generated compound type is $C_{12}A_7$ (C = CaO; A =Al_2O_3) then melting point of this type of component is within the range of steel making temperature.

We form $C_{12}A_7$ type component by injecting Ca- Si wire with 30% Ca to modify melting point of inclusion type Al_2O_3.

- **Specify the roles of "Ca ", "S "and "Al "in enhancing cleanliness and cast ability.**

Ca, S and Al play a major role in cleanliness and cast ability. During steel making Al react with O and develop compound   **Al_2O_3**for improving oxide cleanliness. But **Al_2O_3** has high melting point. This alumina is a solid inclusion in liquid steel. And due to surface tension alumina grow in size. And another reaction takes place during Ca react with S and generates CaS, and decrease sulphure level in liquid steel.

Small large inclusion is very dangerous for steel from the cleanliness aspect. So we try to keep those solid alumina inclusions in liquid stage in the steel making temperature. But melting point of alumina is much higher than the steel making temperature. So to keep those harmful large solid alumina inclusions in liquid stage we use Ca

From Ca, alumina and S phase diagram we find to keep those alumina inclusions in liquid stage both alumina and S both should be low. And more over if we going add on Ca then this Ca react with S and generate CaS which is again solid inclusion that affects cleanliness of steel.

- o **Mention the factors which favor inclusion floatation and absorption in slag of ladle.**

During steel secondary steel making inclusion floatation and absorption depend on following factors

- Inert gas purging provided from bottom of the ladle.
- Size of inclusions and density of inclusion
- Partial pressure for gaseous inclusion
- Amount of surface active element like O and S
- Basicity of slag

How above mentions parameter affects inclusion floatation and absorption in slag of ladle

- Inert gas purging from the bottom of ladle helps to keep liquid steel homogeneous and floatation of inclusion in a rapid manner.
- Size of inclusion plays a major role for floatation and absorption of inclusion in slag of ladle.
  'Ostwal ripening' causes larger particles at cost of smaller one facilitated by surface tension
  From stoke'slaw : velocity $\sim R^2(D_i - D_s)$
  Hence floatation velocity is higher for larger radius and lower density.
- For gaseous inclusion like H and N, it's dependent on partial pressure. Lower the partial pressure higher the consumption
- For the gaseous inclusion like N, it is also dependent on amount of surface active element present in the liquid steel.
- For inclusion like S , it is dependent on basicity of slag.

- ## What are the common sources of large exogenous entrapments in steel?

Different source of large exogenous entrapment in steel

- During steel making at secondary stage.
- Comes from erosion of ladle walls, tundish wall are lined with refractory material.
- Slag from ladle, tundish, mould.
- Reoxidation during casting process.

During steel making at secondary stage alumina is generated and this alumina increase in size due to ostwal ripening. If enough purging time is not provided, there may be entrapment of large inclusions.

Large inclusion may also come from the erosion of ladle walls and tundish walls are line with refractory.

Slag may be entrapped during the casting process when metal coms from ladle to tundish, tundish to mould.

Large inclusion may also develop during casting process. If the is no ladle free opening, we have to do lancing at that time steel gets oxidized. Large inclusion may develop. And during casting if we do not use refractory shroud and SEN then also steel may get oxidized and large inclusion may entrapped. And finally in the mould during casting due to mould fluctuation.

- **Specifically explain how "re-oxidation "of liquid steel can be minimized.**

After the secondary refining possible area of re-oxidation is as follows

- Reaction with refractory material.
- During liquid metal transfer from ladle to tundish.
- In the tundish

- During liquid metal transfer from tundish to mould.

Re-oxidation of liquid steel can be minimized

- ❖ **For reaction with refractory material:** if refractory materials contain oxide element likeSiO_2, NaO_2, K_2O, Fe_2O_3 and percent of Carbon should be less in the refractory. Because in high temperature oxide element will react with carbon of the refractory and will generate oxide and (CO) gas and again (CO) will react with [Al] and will cause to generate **Al_2O_3,** re-oxidation takes place. And refractory get affected.
  So we can minimize reoxidation from refractory material by choosing basic refractory with lower carbon
- ❖ **During liquid metal transfer from ladle to tundish:** During liquid metal transfer from ladle to tundish there may not be a ladle free opening then we have to lance for opening at that time liquid metal gets oxidize.
  After the opening if liquid metal is transferred from ladle to tundish open to air then there also O and N pick-up in liquid metal.
  So we use refractory shroud and argon shroud.
- ❖ **In the tundish:**tundish reoxidation can be minimized by maintaining basic slag and basic refractory.

❖ **During liquid metal transfer from tundish to mould:** we can minimize reoxidation by using sub entry nozzle with argon shrouding.

o **Mention the steps necessary to maintain and enhance the cleanliness level in tundish.**

➢ Use of refractory shroud with argon shroud in ladle for transferring of liquid metal from ladle to tundish to prevent oxygen and nitrogen pick up.
➢ Use of SEN for transferring liquid metal from tundish to mould with argon shroud to prevent oxygen and nitrogen pick up.
➢ Deep immersion of ladle shroud to prevent oxygen and nitrogen pick up.
➢ Prevention of slag carries over from ladle to tundish.
➢ Use of basic refractory free of oxide element and less carbon.
➢ Allowing some residence time to liquid metal. i.e. liquid metal should be allowed to remain in tundish to float up.
➢ Use of dam for creating a circuitous flow of liquid steel allowing some residence time to float up inclusions.
➢ Maintaining basic slag cover in tundish.

➤ Percent of carbon in rice husk insulating type cover of tundish.

o **Explain the processing factors in CC mould which can impair steel cleanliness.**

- SEN configuration and optimal submergence.
- Flow-ability and type of casting powder. Granulated type casting powder with good flow ability helps to improve steel cleanliness.
- Mould slag viscosity.
- Mould level fluctuation.
- Sudden change in casting speed.

o **Explain why cleanliness level in cast slab / bloom is not uniform along its length and thickness.**

cleanliness level and distribution in cast slab or bloom is dependent on different phase of casting.

➤ **Start and end of casting.**
➤ **Ladle change over.**
➤ **Steady state casting.**
➤ **Mould level fluctuation.**

At the start of the casting there is a possibility of re-oxidation of liquid metal, increasing inclusion level in the cast product.

At the end of the casting process there is a possibility of tundish slag entrapment in the liquid metal, decreasing cleanliness of the cast product.

During the ladle change over there is a possibility of ladle slag entrapment in the liquid metal, increasing the level of inclusion in the cast products.

During steady state casting there is also a possibility of mould slag entrapment due to improper characteristics of mould power. It is totally dependent on viscosity or interfacial tension of liquid flux. And there is also a possibility of liquid flux entrapment due to turbulence of liquid metal in the mould that is depending on the design of the SEN.

Again if there is sudden change in casting speed, there is a possibility of increasing turbulence in the liquid metal in the mould. There is also a chance of increasing level of inclusion.

- **Clearly explain the effect of "curved mould "on distribution of inclusion along thickness of cast slab , and explain the distribution in case of " vertical mould " .**

<u>**Curved mould:**</u> In the carved mould during the initial stages of casting solidification starts from the mould to inner side. In the inner radius of the mould there is also a solid shell growth. And the inclusions start to float up. Because of the curvature of the mould inclusions get entrap in the solid shell resulting less inclusions in the outer radius of the caster. So inclusions are more in the top surface of the cast product and decreasing with the thickness of the cast product.

<u>**Vertical mould:**</u> In the vertical mould inclusion in the liquid metal float up straight upward and get absorbed by the mould slag. So there is nearly a uniform distribution of inclusion is possible.

- o **Mention the different possible quality aberrations in cast steel.**

Mainly possible quality aberrations in the cast steel are

- ➢ **Surface imperfections.**
- ➢ **NDT failure.**

Those problem are mainly originating from

- ➢ Poor cleanliness.
- ➢ Surface, subsurface, internal defects (Those are mainly related to steel grade and casting process).

o **What are the major factors which influence the quality issues in cast steel?**

Influence of different factor on cast quality:

- ➢ **Pin hole & Blow hole.**
- ➢ **Surface imperfections.**
- ➢ **Sub-surface defects.**
- ➢ **Internal defects.**

Pin hole and Blow hole: It is generated due to percentage of gaseous element present in the molten steel. Solubility of solute is more in liquid state than solid state. If the percentage of gaseous element present in the liquid steel is more than the solubility limit of solid steel then those gases try to gets out during solidification. Pin hole and Blow hole are generated.

Surface imperfection: surface imperfection occurs depending on steel grade and casting process.

There may be a oscillation marks or depression depending on the steel grade. Oscillation marks are generated due to sticking tendency.

Sub- Surface defects: sub surface defects arise in bend mould Due to floatation of inclusions during casting.

Internal defects: It is generated due to entrapment of mould slag, gaseous bubble entrapment and segregation of solute. Solubility of solute is more in liquid steel than the solubility in solid steel. So during solidification solutes try to get towards the liquid metal so segregation takes place and depending on the cleanliness level of steel defects arise.

- o **How thickness of solid shell increases with time or depth of solidification?**

Solidification of liquid steel starts in the mould. Mould is water cool. Heat flux is taken out from liquid steel by water circulation in the mould. This is called primary cooling.

Then water or mist is sprayed for further cooling. This is called secondary cooling.

Additionally support roll is provided to prevent bending of strip or billet due to Ferro static pressure.

Grain growth start from the surface, when this solidified shell gets out of mould due to secondary cooling thickness of solidified shell starts to grow towards the center of the cast billet, strip or bloom

- o **Quantitatively explain the factors responsible for formation of pin holes in casting.**

It is generated due to percentage of gaseous element present in the molten steel. Solubility of solute is more in liquid state than solid state. If the percentage of gaseous element present in the liquid steel is more than the solubility limit of solid steel then those gases try to gets out during solidification. Pin hole and Blow hole are generated.

$$[H_H] = K_H (P_{H2})^{1/2} \, , \, [H_N] = K_N (P_{N2})^{1/2} \, , \, [H_C] [H_O] = K_{CO} \, P_{CO}$$

Partial pressure can be calculated from weight percent of H, N, and CO. and from the K value at certain temperature.

Total partial pressure $P_{Total} = P_{H2} + P_{N2} + P_{CO}$

Gas bubble form if $P_{Total} > P_{atm} + P_{ferro}$

- o **Explain the parameters which control heat transfer during primary cooling in caster.**

In the mould liquid slag gets drawn into gap between mould and solid shell. Part of slag freezes in contact with cold surface of copper mould.

Heat transfer rate is dependent on relative thickness of solid layer and liquid slag layer in the gap between mould and solidifying shell control.

Important parameters for solidification of liquid slag are basicity and solidification temperature of slag.

High solidification temperature increase solid layer, high basicity facilities crystallization. Both lead to higher heat transfer.

Formation of air gap in case of shrinkage lower heat transfer.

- o **Explain how depth of oscillation mark is influenced by different casting parameters.**

Here we find From the velocity diagram of mould and casting speed , oscillation marks is dependent on negative strip time(t_n) i.e cycle time for $V_m < V_c$

V_m = Velocity of mould.

V_c = velocity of casting.

When $V_m < V_c$ then oscillation marks is generated.

Deep oscillation marks is related to high negative strip time (t_n).

- ➢ **(t_n) will be less if casting speed is slightly higher.**
- ➢ **If the frequency of mould is slightly higher, (t_n) will be lower.**
- ➢ **Lower amplitude of mould.**

- **How and why dendritic arm spacing changes from surface to interior of a casting?**

If we look at the solid structure of a cast product we found three type of dendrite formation. First we find fine grain equiaxed dendrite then columnar dendrite then we may or may not find equiaxed depending on the superheat temperature.

Surface chilled zone- equiaxed dendrite structure- we find this layer for a few mm of cast product surface or only for a fraction of second during casting due to chilling effect.

Columnar dendrite zone- Then after some time of casting columnar type of dendritic grain growth starts.

Central equiaxed zone- we may or may not find equiaxed depending on the superheat temperature and segregation.

- **Explain how to ensure desirable distribution of columnar and equiaxed cast grains.**

Alloying elements are rejected from solid to liquid during solidification due to segregation.

Solidification starts as a plane front but soon changed into dendritic type due to constitutional super cooling.

Super cooling is due to enrichment of liquid with more solutes due to segregations.

Cast structure – columnar + equiaxed

> - **% of equiaxed is respectively large with low superheat and EMS.**
> - **Higher cooling rate at surface results in finer dendrite spacing.**
> - **With 20⁰C superheat casting we find 20% to 30% equiaxed dendrite in central zone.**
> - **With 50⁰C superheat casting we find columnar dendrites growth up to center of the cast product.**

- o **Explain the sequence of solidification for steels with 0.05, 0.20 and 0.60 % carbon.**

For solidification sequence of steel we follow pseudo iron-carbon diagram.

The liquid may transform into Ferrite **– δ and Austenite – γ**

Possible routes are

> - **Liquid to δ**
> - **Liquid to δ + γ**
> - **Liquid to γ**

We can calculate those routes by ferrite potential.

Ferrite potential (FP) = 2.5 (0.5 – Carbon equivalent)

C_{eq} = C+ 0.04 Mn+ 0.7N- 0.14Si – 0.04Cr-0.1 Mo – 0.24 Ti

Solidification sequence if

FP > 1   **δ solidification mode.**

FP > 1   **δ + γ solidification mode.**

FP > 1   **γ solidification mode.**

For steel with 0.05 % carbon solidification mode will be through **L to L + δ then δ finally γ**

For steel with 0.20 % carbon solidification mode will be through **L to L + δ then L + δ + γ finally γ**

For steel with 0.60 % carbon solidification mode will be through **L to L + γ then γ.**

> o **Identify at what stage transformation occurs in the above three steels.**

For steel with 0.05 % carbon solidification mode will be through **L to L + δ then δ finally γ. Transformation from δ to γ takes place in solid state.**

For steel with 0.20 % carbon solidification mode will be through **L to L + δ then L + δ + γ finally γ.**

Transformation from δ to γ takes place in liquid state.

For steel with 0.60 % carbon solidification mode will be through **L to L + γ then γ. Here solidification is only in γ mode.**

- o **Why "S "or "P "segregates more during solidification than "Mn "or "Si "?**

Micro segregation during solidification results in increase in concentration of an alloying element from original value of C_0 in liquid steel to higher value of the same element in last solidifying liquid C_L

$C_L = C_0 [1-F_s/(ak+1)]^{k-1}$ Back   diffusion
parameter a= $D_s * T_f(L/2)^{-2}$

K is distribution coefficient of alloying element between solid and liquid.

Lower value of partition coefficient k and diffusion coefficient in solid D_s for an alloying element result in higher enrichment C_L

value of distribution coefficient (k) is lower for "S" and "P" than "Mn" and "Si". That's why "S" and "P" segregates more during solidification.

- o **How segregation changes the "actual solidus "of steel, and the relative depths of "solid Shell "and "mushy zone" in the solidifying strand?**

Micro segregation during solidification results in increase in concentration of an alloying element from original value of C_0 in liquid steel to higher value of the same element in last solidifying liquid C_L

$C_L = C_0 [1-F_s/(ak+1)]^{k-1}$ Back   diffusion
parameter a$= D_s * T_f(L/2)^{-2}$

Lower value of partition coefficient k and diffusion coefficient in solid D_s for an alloying element result in higher enrichment C_L

Higher C_L actual solidus T_{SA} comes down from the equilibrium solidus $T_{SE.}$ so actual temperature range of solidification (T_L-T_{SA}) increases.

This leads to **higher actual depth of mushy zone (S+ L) and lower actual thickness of solid shell.**

○ **Mention the sources of strains on the cast strand during and after solidification.**

Different source of strain on cast strand during solidification.

- For ferostatic force from liquid during solidification
- For shrinkage due to solidification and transformation from δ to γ.
- Mechanical strain due to bending and unbending of strand.
- Thermal strain during secondary cooling.

And after solidification there is no strain.

○ **Explain the significance of " ZST " , " ZDT " and " LIT " of the strand during casting .**

ZST- Zero Strain Temperature
          at solid fraction- 0.75
ZDT- Zero Ductility Temperature
          at solid fraction- 1.0
LIT- Liquid Impenetrable Temperature
          at solid fraction- 0.9

During solidification dendrite growth before complete solidification some mechanical property develop

At solid fraction 0.75 some toughness is generated this temperature is called zero strain temperature.

At solid fraction 0.1 ductility is developed this temperature is called zero strain temperature.

During solidification due to external mechanical strain if some crack is developed in crystal, liquid steel can heal up the cracks of dendrite up to the solid fraction 0.9 this temperature is called liquid impenetrable temperature.

- o **Why knowledge of both strength and toughness of solidifying strand is important**

Knowledge of strength and toughness is important because we need to bending and straightening during casting to bring the final product horizontal.

And there also many several strain during solidification.

- For ferostatic force from liquid during solidification
- For shrinkage due to solidification and transformation from δ to γ.

- Mechanical strain due to bending and unbending of strand.
- Thermal strain during secondary cooling.

During solidification dendrite growth before complete solidification some mechanical property develop

At solid fraction 0.75 some toughness is generated this temperature is called zero strain temperature.

At solid fraction 0.1 ductility is developed this temperature is called zero strain temperature.

During solidification due to external mechanical strain if some crack is developed in crystal, liquid steel can heal up the cracks of dendrite up to the solid fraction 0.9 this temperature is called liquid impenetrable temperature.

○ **Clearly specify the importance of "brittle zone near actual solidus "on crack formation during solidification.**

ZST- Zero Strain Temperature
     at solid fraction- 0.75

ZDT- Zero Ductility Temperature
    at solid fraction- 1.0

LIT- Liquid Impenetrable Temperature
    at solid fraction- 0.9

During solidification dendrite growth before complete solidification some mechanical property develop

At solid fraction 0.75 some toughness is generated this temperature is called zero strain temperature.

At solid fraction 0.1 ductility is developed this temperature is called zero strain temperature.

During solidification due to external mechanical strain if some crack is developed in crystal, liquid steel can heal up the cracks of dendrite up to the solid fraction 0.9 this temperature is called liquid impenetrable temperature.

Brittle zone near actual solidus when solid fraction is within 0.9 to 1. In this range chance of crack formation increase as this is very brittle and again there is no chance of crack penetration by liquid steel.

- ○ **Mention how the two essential intrinsic solidification behaviors are related to actual casting factors.**

Two opposing forces are acting on solid shell

- **Ferrostaticforce push solid shell towards mould.**

  Sticking/ Bulging strain $S_B = F/\sigma\ S_A^2$

  F is ferrostatic force

σ is strength of shell

S_A is the actual shell thickness.

- Shrinkage due solidification cooling and transformation from δ to γ.
  Thermal strain $S_{TH} = \beta(T_{SA} - T_O)$
  β is coefficient of thermal expansion.
- Transformation strain S_{TR} is relevant only in brittle temp zone LIT to T_{SA}.

➤ $S_B > (S_{TR} + S_{TH})$ results in sticking & bulging tendency.

➤ $S_B < (S_{TR} + S_{TH})$ results in formation of surface depression.

o **Why "P "is more deleterious for steel grades solidifying through γ than δ**

Micro segregation during solidification results in increase in concentration of an alloying element from original value of C_0 in liquid steel to higher value of the same element in last solidifying liquid C_L

$C_L = C_0 [1-F_s/(ak+1)]^{k-1}$ Back   diffusion
parameter a= $D_s * T_f(L/2)^{-2}$

     K is distribution coefficient of alloying element

between solid and
liquid.

Lower value of partition coefficient k for an alloying element result in higher enrichment C_L.

High Mn/ S (>25) can control deleterious effect of S but there is no such element to take care of P

In case of γ solidification distribution coefficient K value of "P" is smaller than δ solidification.

- **Explain for which carbon content strain associated with δ to γ transformation is a matter of**

Solidification mode is dependent on carbon equivalent in steel. δ to γ transformation also dependent on carbon equivalent in steel and at what stage transformation takes place.

Near about 0.15% carbon equivalent high strain due to solidification cooling and transformation at brittle zone generating high strain.

> Brittle zone near actual solidus when solid fraction is within 0.9 to 1. In this range chance of crack formation increase as this is very brittle and again there is no chance of crack penetration by liquid steel.

- **How chemistry of a steel grade influences its intrinsic solidification characteristic**

Solidification characteristics is totally dependent on chemistry of steel or C_{eq} of the steel.

Parameters	0.02-0.05% C_{eq}	Peritectic ~ 0.1% C_{eq}	0.2-0.4% C_{eq}	> 0.5% C_{eq}
Solidification mode	Entirely δ	δ till Fs~ 0.75, δ + γ at Fs~ 0.8-1.0	δ till Fs~ 0.3, δ +γ at Fs~ 0.3-0.5	Entirely γ
Solid shell	Thick but weak	Thick an strong	Thin	Thin but strong
Mushy zone	Narrow	Narrow	Deep	Deep
δ to γ around solidus	-	High	-	-
Mould sticking	High	-	High	High
Bulging	High	-	High	High
Depression	-	High	-	-

- ✓ **If δ to γ transformation is near solidus then there is shrinkage this type of grade is a depression type grade.**
- ✓ **And if the δ to γ transformation is in solid state then there is thick shell thick ness but due to weak shell it cannot with withstand Ferro static force so this is a sticking type of grade.**
- ✓ **If total solidification through γ then there is a wide mushy zone so shell thickness is less. So due to Ferro static force this type of grade is a sticking type grade.**

- o **What are the factors responsible for generation of cracks on concast surface?**

Surface Crack – Related to uneven shell growth (Mainly for striker type of grades).

- ➢ Longitudinal at mid face and near corner locations on billet/ bloom/ slab and all rounds for round section.
- ➢ Mainly coinciding with longitudinal depression.
- ➢ Transverse cracks primarily related to deep oscillation marks and transverse

depression (can be controlled by controlling negative strip time).

Internal crack – Related to inter dendritic hot tears caused by strain in the solidifying shell exceeding critical limit.

- o **Explain why some times undesirable "coarse cast grains "are formed.**

There are mainly two categories of steel grade as per solidification type- **striker type and depression type.**
Grain size is totally dependent on heat transfer rate and mode of solidification δ and γ. Higher the heat transfer finer the grain size.
The steel grade with C_{eq} ~ 0.1% is a depression type of grade. In this type of grade during casting there is a additional shrinkage due to δ to γ transformation near solidus. So there is chance of developing air gap between mould surfaces and solidifying shell. So heat transfer gets affected. So there Coarse cast grains is found.

- o **Specify the factors associated with the different temperature regions of brittleness.**

During casting there are several brittle zones.

Measure of brittleness – when there is low reduction in area (<50% area reduction.)

Solidifying shell during cooling undergoes three brittle zones.

> **Around and bellow actual solidus(till 50⁰C below of f_s =1)**
>
> Stress in this zone will generate inter-columnar crack.

> **Around 1000 – 1100⁰C**
>
> Segregation of P, S, O along inter – granular austenite.

> **Around 600 -700⁰C**
>
> Precipitation of nitrite of Al, Nb, V along coarse γ grains.

○ **Mention the common internal cracks in continuous casting and their reasons.**

> **Surface Defects**
>
> - Longitudinal mid face cracks.
> - Longitudinal surface cracks.
> - Longitudinal corner cracks.
> - Longitudinal off corner cracks.
> - Transverse corner cracks.
> - Transverse surface cracks.
> - Fine cracks.

> **Internal Defects**
>   - Longitudinal corner cracks.
>   - Longitudinal off corner cracks.
>   - Halfway crack.
>   - Spider crack.
>   - Central crack.

Surface Crack – Related to uneven shell growth (Mainly for striker type of grades).

> ➢ Longitudinal at mid face and near corner locations on billet/ bloom/ slab and all rounds for round section.
> ➢ Mainly coinciding with longitudinal depression.
> ➢ Transverse cracks primarily related to deep oscillation marks and transverse depression (can be controlled by controlling negative strip time).

Internal crack – Related to inter dendritic hot tears caused by strain in the solidifying shell exceeding critical limit.

- **How bulging in cast slab can be controlled in mould, and during secondary cooling.**

Controlling method for bulging type of grade.

In the Mould: In depressing type of bulging is the main problem. That can be controlled by using proper casting powder. Depending on casting powder the relative thickness of mould slag and air gap between mould and solid shell is dependent. And depending on the thickness of mould slag heat transfer is dependent.

During secondary cooling: During secondary cooling it is totally dependent on intensity of secondary cooling. Depending on cooling intensity temperature of solid shell surface is reached. And depending on shell temperature total γ is dependent. As strength of γ is five times of δ so depending on cooling intensity the strength of solid shell is dependent.

Depending on grade of steel we have to set casting parameter like casting speed, casting powder, secondary cooling intensity etc.

o **Specify why steels solidifying "entirely through δ or γ "are prone to mould sticking.**

Two opposing forces are acting on solid shell

- **Ferro static force push solid shell towards mould.**
  Sticking/ Bulging strain $S_B = F/\sigma\, S_A^2$
  F is Ferro static force
  σ is strength of shell
  S_A is the actual shell thickness.

- Shrinkage due solidification cooling and transformation from δ to γ.
    Thermal strain $S_{TH} = \beta(T_{SA} - T_O)$
    β is coefficient of thermal expansion.
  - Transformation strain S_{TR} is relevant only in brittle temp zone LIT to T_{SA}.

➤ $S_B > (S_{TR} + S_{TH})$ results in sticking & bulging tendency.

➤ $S_B < (S_{TR} + S_{TH})$ results in formation of surface depression.

  - ✓ **Here S_B is dependent on σ and σ is dependent on δ and γ. For γ mode solidification σ value is five times.**
  - ✓ **Again if δ to γ transformation is near solidus then there is shrinkage this type of grade is a depression type grade.**
  - ✓ **And if the δ to γ transformation is in solid state or total solidification through γ then there is a wide mushy zone so shell thickness is less. So due to Ferro static force this type of grade is a sticking type grade.**

o **Specify the CC parameters necessary for good quality irrespective of steel grade.**

Irrespective of steel grade casting parameters are:

> **Speed and superheat**- Depending upon the speed of caster mould level fluctuation depends and also the probability of slag entrapment depends. Also depression marks depends. And grain size depends on the super heat.

> **Mould Lubrication-** Mould lubrication is the main important thing in the casting process otherwise liquid metal will stick with mould wall so casting powder with proper viscosity and lubrication is important.

> **Secondary cooling-** Strength of solid shell depend on thickness of the solid shell. Higher the intensity of cooling higher the strength of solid shell.

> **Powder Characteristics** – Powder characteristics plays a crucial role during casting. Heat transfer in the mould depends on the powder characteristics.

> **Mould oscillation and setting-** Depending on the mould oscillation depression on marks or crack under the depression marks depends. Proper setting is necessary.

> **SEN configuration and submergence-** Proper SEN configuration and proper submergence are necessary to avoid

turbulence in mould and slag entrainment in cast product.

> **Caster type-** Depending on the caster type curved mould or straight mould inclusion distribution depends.
> **Distribution of Strain-** Strain distribution in the caster plays a crucial role in casting process. For the excess mechanical strain in solid shell there is a possibility of crack formation.

o **Which parameters are essential for the so-called peritectic grade with about 0.1% C?**

Peritectic grade with about 0.1% C is a depression type of grade.

Location and Direction of Defects (Crack)

✓ Longitudinal at mid-face and near corner location on billet/bloom/slab, and all around for the round section.
✓ Mainly coinciding with longitudinal depression.
✓ Transverse crack primarily related to deep oscillation marks and transverse depression.

Essential parameters for peritectic grade:

- ✓ Lower C_{eq} in peritectic grades avoids δ to γ in brittle zone control longitudinal crack and depression and coarse γ.
- ✓ Minimum Residuals- Lower N, Al in peritectic grades restrict AlN precipitation at coarse γ boundary thereby control transverse crack.
- ✓ Mould slag with lower heat transfer for peritectic grades.

- ○ **Explain why "mechanical soft reduction "is desirable to minimize central looseness.**

  Central line defects only can be controlled by
  - ✓ Controlling low segregation
  - ✓ Low superheats casting (More equiaxed zone at center).
  - ✓ Mechanical soft reduction.

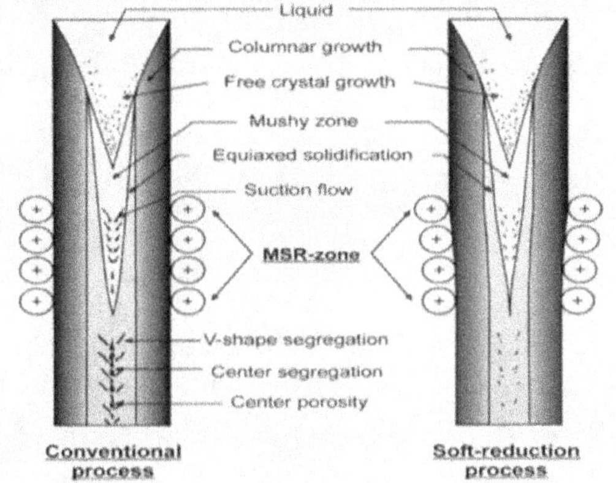

Mechanical soft reduction process

We use this process to control central defects. In this process we apply the compression along the thickness. We gradually increase the compression form near solidus to final solidification of central regio

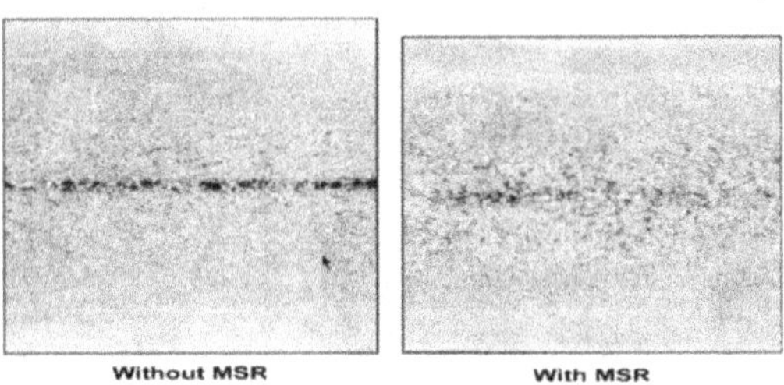

n.

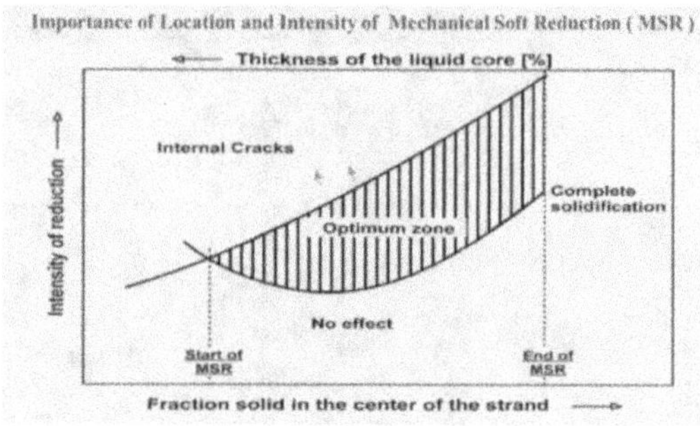

If we apply very much load that can also create crack and if we apply very low intensity of load then also there we will not get desired result. So we have to apply proper intensity and proper solidification location in a gradually increasing manner then only we can get desired result.

In conventional Process
- ✓ V shape segregation.
- ✓ Center segregation
- ✓ Center porosity

After Soft reduction
- ✓ Compensating final shrinkage.
- ✓ Absence of porosity
- ✓ Absence of crack

o **Why higher ratio (> 25) of Mn / S in steel is desirable for good quality?**

Micro segregation during solidification results in increase in concentration of an alloying element from original value of C_o in liquid steel to higher value of the same element in last solidifying liquid C_L

C_L = C0 [1-Fs/(ak+1)]k-1   Back
diffusion parameter a= Ds * Tf(L/2)-2
K is distribution coefficient of alloying element between solid and liquid.
- ✓ Lower value of partition coefficient k for an alloying element result in higher enrichment C_L.
- ✓ High Mn/ S (>25) can control deleterious effect of S.
- ✓ In case of γ solidification distribution coefficient K value of "P" is smaller than δ solidification.
- ✓ Lower P, S and higher Mn/S in austenitic grades restrict micro segregation, increase shell thickness, control central segregation.

o **Why casting powder of different characteristics are used for AISI 430 and AISI 304?**

- ✓ AISI304 is a peritectic grade.
- ✓ AISI430 is a ferritic steel.

Solidification mode is different for those two type of grade. Solidification mode is δ to γ transformation takes place near solidus. But for ferritic grade AISI403 δ to γ takes place in solid state.

So for ferritic grade
- ✓ Shell is thick but weak.
- ✓ Sticking and bulging tendency.

For peritectic grade
- ✓ Shell is thick and strong.
- ✓ Depression type of grade.

Casting powder specification:
> - Mould slag with better lubrication for sticking type of grades.
> - Mould slag with lower heat transfer for depression grade.
> - Higher secondary cooling to control bulging in very low carbon ferritic grade.

o **How the genesis of undesirable entrapments in steel can be specifically found out?**

There are various sources of undesirable entrapments in steel like ladle, tundish or mould

A few large inclusions are very dangerous so we have to be very careful about exogenous entrapment.

For the details study of entrapment we use elemental microanalysis of entrapment by secondary electron microscope.

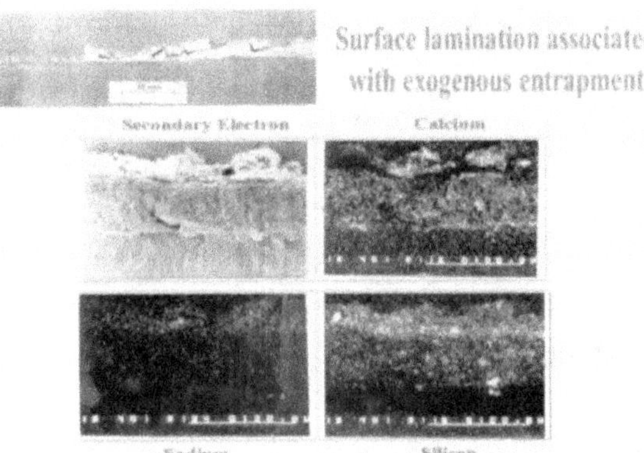

- ✓ **If we find calcium oxide then we can assume that probable entrapment genesis from ladle during ladle change over.**
- ✓ **If we find silicon oxide in the entrapment then we can assume that probable entrapment genesis from tundish slag because tundish slag is in rich of Si due to rise husk.**
- ✓ **If we find sodium oxide then we can assume that probable entrapment genesis from mould slag due to turbulence or mould level fluctuation.**

- o **Explain the features revealed by simple polishing and those by subsequent etching.**

In case of quality inspection of continuous cast steel we know it by methodology of investigation.

Firstly we inspect product to identify location, size, shape, frequency of occurrence of defects.

Then we preserving and observing the defect with naked eye or magnifying glass.

Then we carefully cut the sample for metallographic observation using optical and SEM in this case transverse section is polished, etched.

Observations:

- ✓ Scale, associated change in microstructure, like grain coarsening, internal oxidation
- ✓ Location of exogenous NMI (normally >100 micron)
- ✓ Elemental information using EDX or WDX to identify chemistry and source of NMI.

Common Defects:

- • **Edge crack**
  - o Chemistry balance of δ and γ

- o Hot rolling parameters, type of HR mill
  - o HR thickness
- **Shell/ Scale**
  - o Near edge- chemistry related.
  - o Only scale and associated microstructural change like internal oxidation, grain coarsening- Defects imparted during HR and Defects existing at subsurface of continuous cast material respectively.
  - o Anywhere along coil width- Large NMI or mechanical damage during CR processing.
- **Sliver/ Slag line**
  - o Entrainment of slag from ladle/ tundish/ mould
- **Tearing or Hole**
  - o Mainly due to cold workability
- **Transverse Crack**
  - o Mainly due to transverse defects existing at surface or subsurface location in cast slab.

Material defects existing at surface or subsurface of cast slab related to chemistry of grade or influence by casting parameter

Entrapment of large exogenous NMI during steel refining or casting related to reoxidation, nozzle clogged product or slag from ladle/ tundish/ mould or refractory erosion.

We can find the elemental by elemental analysis by SEM

There are various sources of undesirable entrapments in steel like ladle, tundish or mould
A few large inclusions are very dangerous so we have to be very careful about exogenous entrapment.
For the details study of entrapment we use elemental microanalysis of entrapment by secondary electron microscope.

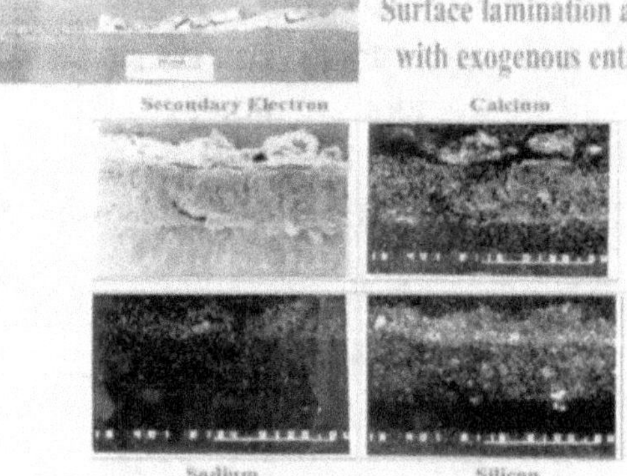

- ✓ **If we find calcium oxide then we can assume that probable entrapment genesis from ladle during ladle change over.**
- ✓ **If we find silicon oxide in the entrapment then we can assume that**

probable entrapment genesis from tundish slag because tundish slag is in rich of Si due to rise husk.
✓ If we find sodium oxide then we can assume that probable entrapment genesis from mould slag due to turbulence or mould level fluctuation.

THANKS

---

www.ingramcontent.com/pod-product-compliance
Lightning Source LLC
Chambersburg PA
CBHW060802260726
48660CB00002B/736